TWO WHEELS EXPOSED

Bicycles in The Land of The Rising Sun

Photographs by Miranda Boller

Printed in the United States of America
First Printing, 2024
ISBN 979-8-9899326-1-0

www.mirandaboller.com

今が旬！
べったら漬

1袋（ハーフサイズ）

税込み **500** 円

サービス

べったら漬

国内産 大根使用

皮付 **1,000** 円

皮なし **800** 円

人気商品！

季節限定品！
旬の味覚！

税込み
200円

本日のお買得

本日のお買得

INTRO

by Miranda Boller

We are surrounded by various objects that play a vital role in improving our daily routine. These objects contribute to making our lives easier and often we go about our day, not even recognizing their significance. For instance, travel incorporates many objects that help us get from point A to point B. Whether it be a plane flying in the air, that train rolling on the track, the public bus, your reliable car, a two wheeled bicycle or those loyal walking shoes, we get to where we want to go in a much more comfortable and smoother way thanks to all these objects.

When you move to another country, and step outside your normal routine you tend to see the world through a different lens. You quickly develop renewed gratitude for the things you no longer have, and you also begin to appreciate the value of things you never used. After living in Los Angeles for eight years, I married the love of my life and moved to Atsugi, Japan, a city on the outskirts of Tokyo.

Coming from a city that lacked efficient public transportation and where I relied heavily on my car, I was more than happy to ditch the four wheels and embrace the city life of walking and taking trains everywhere.

As I took the time to slow down and discover Japan by foot, I instantly noticed the ubiquitous presence of bicycles. I was constantly intrigued by how these bicycles were fully exposed to every passerby and often they were not even locked up. With the culture of trust and low-crime in Japan, this may have been common to many, but to me, a foreigner getting lost in a new unknown territory, it came as quite a shock.

I kept capturing photographs of each bicycle I encountered because I loved how they were a part of their environment. These two wheels would be resting carefree against a building, home, pole or wall ready to contribute when called upon. I found myself constantly asking questions. How long had it been sitting there? What role did it play in its owner's life? What was its story? I knew these questions would never be answered, but my imagination began to explode with a variety of different stories. These bicycles spoke to me through their simple act of being exposed and gently reminded me of the importance of objects that surround us every day.

This book is a compilation of my favorite bicycle photographs I took throughout Japan. I hope that they ignite a feeling within you, one similar to what ignited me to capture these images and publish this book. As a passerby, I was just a fragment in each bicycle's story but I hope together we can create a much bigger story. One that connects us and brings us together through the extraordinary beauty of ordinary objects.

Dedicated to:

Douglas & Françoise Kirkland

For all you two taught me about

photography, art and living

the most beautiful life possible.

クリーヌ

OPEN 10時30分〜18時30分 ☎03・6231

ご拝観の皆様へ
こちらから東福寺への
車両（タクシー）乗り入
れはご遠慮下さい。

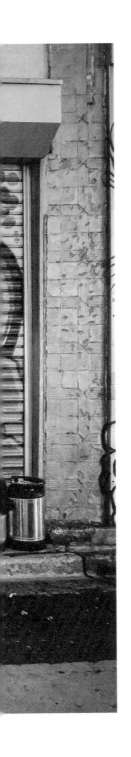

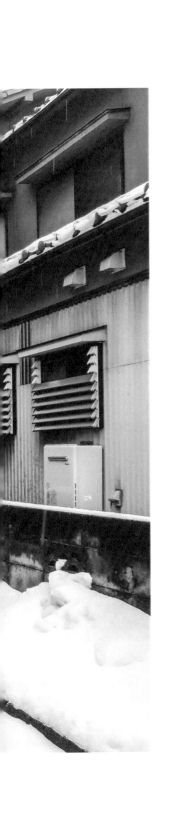